Magic Mixtures

Creative Fun for Little Ones
Preschool–Grade 3

by Jean Stangl

Fearon Teacher Aids
Carthage, Illinois

ISBN 0-8224-4377-5

Library of Congress Catalog Card Number: 85-80254

Printed in the United States of America

1. 9 8 7 6

Contents

Introduction

The early childhood years—the creative years—find the young child eager to explore, investigate, and manipulate. The added tactile experience of creative mixtures encourages exploration, stimulates the imagination, and aids in concept development.

The projects in *Magic Mixtures: Creative Fun for Little Ones* are meant to be creative experiences. Therefore, it is important to allow children time and freedom to create. Be sure to pretest all recipes before introducing them to the children, and make sure you have all necessary ingredients, containers, and utensils. Adjust the recipes as necessary to accommodate the size of your group. Involve the students as much as possible by having them participate in gathering materials, measuring, mixing, and cleaning up. It is a good idea to supply aprons, smocks, or old shirts to protect the children's clothing.

While children are involved in the activities, encourage them to converse, share observations, verbalize procedures, and discuss the feel, smell, and taste (when appropriate) of the mixtures.

Although this book contains recipes for art experiences, it is not limited to that part of the curriculum. There is great therapeutic value in using the hands to work with a pliable mixture. As the mixture takes form, the child will experience an increased sense of self-esteem and confidence.

Young children will become aware of textures, solids, liquids, and changes in color. They will discover what happens when various materials are combined. They will also discover that thick mixtures are hard to stir and thin mixtures are easy. Learning how to thicken and thin the mixtures and seeing how materials change when they are cooked will be exciting experiences for your students.

Magic Mixtures: Creative Fun for Little Ones is a valuable resource that gives directions and recipes for easy-to-make creative materials. The wide choice of multisensory experiences and activities will make learning and discovering fun for young children.

Young children learn best by being actively involved in a project, and these "magic creations" will provide numerous opportunities for experimenting, exploring, discovering, and learning.

Note: Some ingredients, such as food coloring or tempera, may stain fabric, furniture, or children. Exercise customary cautions.

Chapter 1

Finger Paint: Uncooked, Cooked, and Edible Paint Mixtures

What Is
Finger Painting?

Finger painting is a natural expression of a person's creativity. Painting with the hands is a therapeutic, multisensory activity that offers a variety of learning and discovering experiences. Students will learn to identify the parts of their hands as they discover that fists, nails, and palms all make different designs. Finger painting can be used to present concepts and to develop basic skills. It is a good way to practice letters and shapes, to do simple math, and to play partner games.

Finger painting is not just for preschoolers. Children of all ages and developmental levels will profit by using this fascinating medium for self-expression.

Through the creative process of finger painting, students will learn about textures. They will also learn about what happens when opaque and transparent colors are mixed. In addition, they will experience the joy and satisfaction that comes from creating with one's hands and fingers.

Glossy paper, such as butcher paper and shelf paper, works best for the beginner. Later, children can experiment with construction paper, paper bags, wallpaper, foil, and other kinds of paper. For group murals, use a continuous sheet of wide paper. The edges of some papers will tend to curl as they dry. If

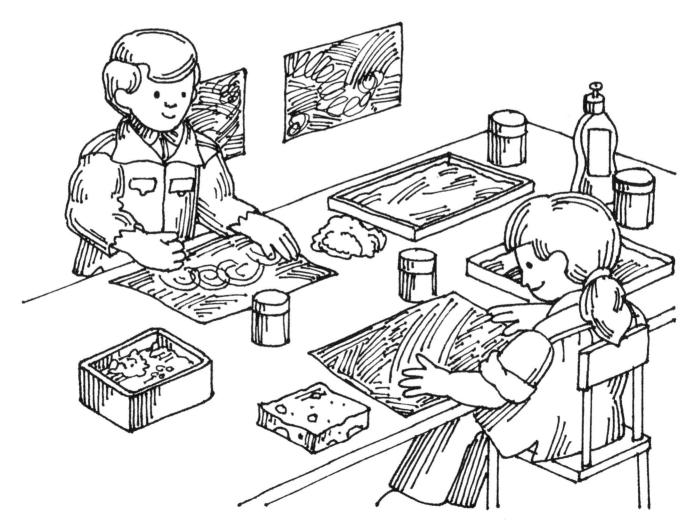

this happens, turn the paper over and press gently with a warm iron.

For an added dimension, mix extracts and spices with the paint mixture. Be sure to have children share in mixing, pouring, and cleaning up. For finger painting activities, you will need a large plastic tray, sponges, a pan of soapy water, paint smocks or old shirts with the sleeves cut off, paper, and paint. Tint paint mixtures, except edible types, with powdered tempera or food coloring. Liquid soap added to the paint will help prevent staining and make it easier to wash out of clothing.

For first experiences, pour the paint into a large plastic tray. Children can take turns painting and creating. To save a design, place a large sheet of paper over the print and press firmly. Carefully lift off and allow to dry.

Do not make samples for the children. Encourage them to experiment with different parts of their hands to make a variety of designs.

Snoopy Loopy

Play this "Snoopy Loopy" game with the children by calling out these directions and having the children follow them as they finger paint.

Snoopy Loopy says,

"Push up with the heel of your hand."

Snoopy Loopy says,

"Make small circles with your thumb."

Snoopy Loopy says,

"Walk your fingers across the paper."

Snoopy Loopy says,

"Make designs by using your fist."

Draw a picture of Snoopy Loopy.
Let the children take turns being Snoopy Loopy and giving directions. Encourage them to make up their own directions.

Uncooked Finger Paints

As an initial introduction to the use of finger paint, a mixture of powdered tempera and liquid starch is probably the most interesting and successful medium. Supply several colors of powdered tempera for the children.

Tempera and Starch #1

⅛ cup liquid starch

1 tablespoon powdered tempera

Supervise as you have children follow these steps:

1. Pour starch directly onto paper.
2. Sprinkle the tempera over the starch.
3. Mix the color in as you paint.

Tempera and Starch #2

2 cups powdered tempera

1 cup liquid starch

water

Supervise as you have children follow these steps:

1. Mix tempera and starch until it is smooth and creamy.
2. Slowly add water until the mixture has a good, thick consistency.

Wheat Paste Paint

1 cup wheat paste
3 tablespoons powdered tempera
water
1 tablespoon soap flakes*
   (optional)
* If you are unable to find soap
   flakes, make your own with a
   kitchen vegetable grater and a
   bar of Ivory soap.

Supervise as you have children
follow these steps:

1. Mix together the wheat paste
   and powdered tempera.
2. Add water until the mixture has
   a creamy consistency.
3. Add soap flakes for smoothness,
   if desired.

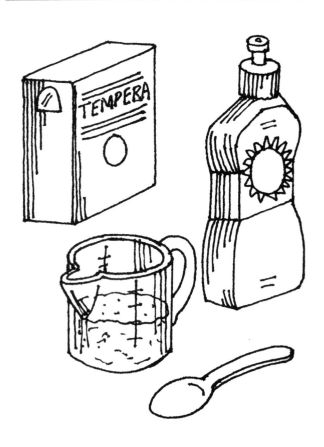

Tempera Detergent Paint

1 cup powdered tempera
4 tablespoons liquid starch
2 teaspoons liquid dish detergent
water

Supervise as you have children
follow these steps:

1. Mix together the first three
   ingredients.
2. Slowly add water until the
   mixture is smooth and creamy.

Dry Starch Paint

1 cup dry laundry starch
1 cup mild soap powder
2 tablespoons powdered tempera
1 cup water

Supervise as you have children follow these steps:

1. Combine all ingredients.
2. Beat the mixture until it is smooth.
3. Add more water if mixture is too thick.

Flour Paint

3 cups flour
2 tablespoons liquid soap
¾ cup water
food coloring or powdered tempera

Supervise as you have children follow these steps:

1. Combine the first three ingredients until the mixture is a thick paste.
2. Tint with food coloring or powdered tempera.

| Liquid Tempera and
Powdered Detergent Paint |
| --- |

5 tablespoons liquid tempera

1 cup powdered detergent

¼ cup water

Supervise as you have children
follow these steps:

1. Combine first two ingredients.
   Add water as necessary.
2. Stir until the mixture is smooth
   and creamy.

Special Ways to Use Finger Paints

For added interest, have children try the
following:

1. Pour any uncooked finger paint mixture
   onto glossy paper. Use an ice cube to
   spread and dilute the paint as you create
   designs.

2. Thoroughly wet a piece of red, black, or
   blue butcher paper with water. Sprinkle 3
   tablespoons of soap flakes on the wet
   paper. Mix the soap flakes and water as
   you finger paint.

Cooked Finger Paints

Make cooked finger paints in the classroom. Use an electric skillet and a long-handled spoon. For recipes that require boiling water, an electric teapot and a mixing bowl would be useful. Cooking activities should be supervised by an adult. Allow paint to cool before the children use it.

Flour Paint

2 cups flour
2 teaspoons salt
3 cups cold water
2 cups hot water
food coloring

Supervise as you have children follow these steps:

1. Mix flour and salt together in an electric skillet.
2. Add cold water and stir until the mixture is smooth.
3. Pour in hot water and bring the mixture to a boil. Boil until it is clear.
4. Add food coloring and beat until smooth.

Dry Laundry Starch

¼ cup dry laundry starch
cold water
2 cups boiling water
food coloring

Supervise as you have children follow these steps:

1. Mix starch with a small amount of cold water to make a paste.
2. Add boiling water and stir until the mixture is thick and clear.
3. Add food coloring.

Dry Starch and Soap Flakes

½ cup dry starch

cold water

1⅓ cups boiling water

½ cup soap flakes*

1 tablespoon glycerine

powdered tempera

* If you are unable to find soap flakes, make your own with a kitchen vegetable grater and a bar of Ivory soap.

Supervise as you have children follow these steps:

1. In an electric skillet, mix starch with enough cold water to make a smooth paste.
2. Add boiling water and stir the mixture on a medium heat setting until it is glossy. Turn heat off.
3. Stir in soap flakes.
4. When the mixture is cool, add glycerine and powdered tempera.

Gelatin Paint

½ cup cornstarch

1 cup cold water

1 envelope plain gelatin

2 cups hot water

½ cup powdered detergent

food coloring or powdered tempera

Supervise as you have children follow these steps:

1. Dissolve cornstarch in ¾ cup cold water.
2. Soak gelatin in remaining ¼ cup cold water.
3. Pour hot water into an electric skillet. Slowly stir cornstarch mixture into the hot water. Stir the mixture on a medium heat setting until it is thick and glossy.
4. Blend gelatin and detergent into the cornstarch mixture. Stir until they dissolve.
5. Add food coloring or powdered tempera.

Edible Finger Paints

Before beginning projects that use edible finger paint mixtures, be sure to have the children wash their hands. Use clean paper or trays, and check with the children to make sure there are no food allergies.

Gelatin Paint

glossy finger paint paper

gelatin (Raspberry, black cherry, and blackberry flavors emit the strongest odors and give the deepest colors.)

water

Supervise as you have children follow these steps:

1. Wet finger paint paper on the glossy side.
2. Sprinkle 2 to 3 tablespoons of dry gelatin on the wet paper.
3. Use as finger paint.

Pudding Paint

6-ounce package instant pudding (chocolate, pistachio, or lemon)

2 cups milk

Supervise as you have children follow these steps:

1. Pour pudding mix and milk into a glass bowl.
2. Beat with a rotary eggbeater until the mixture is thick.
3. Spoon the pudding onto paper. Use as finger paint.

Another way for children to mix this is to place the pudding and milk in a jar, cover the jar with a tight-fitting lid, and shake it until the mixture is thick.

This is an interesting experience because when the child starts to paint, the mixture feels grainy, then it becomes slippery, then it becomes sticky, and when it dries it will again feel grainy.

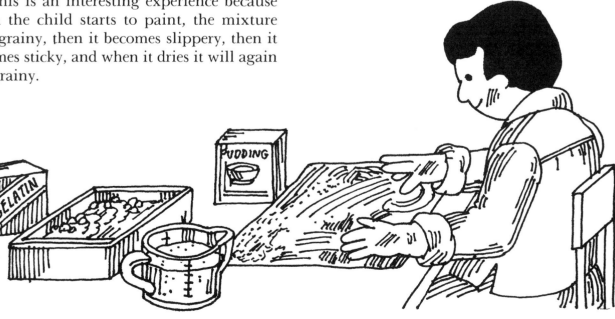

Canned Cake Frosting	Dessert Toppings

Canned Cake Frosting

prepared frosting mix
glossy paper

Supervise as you have children follow these steps:

1. Spoon prepared frosting mix onto glossy paper.
2. Use as finger paint.

Have children use light-colored frosting on dark papers and dark-colored frosting on white papers.

Dessert Toppings

dessert toppings (frozen or in aerosol cans)
finger paint paper
food coloring

Supervise as you have children follow these steps:

1. Spoon or spray dessert topping directly onto the paper.
2. Tint the topping with a few drops of food coloring.

Extended Ideas for Finger Painting

After your students have had ample opportunities to experiment with finger painting as an art, have them cover a large, heavy sheet of butcher paper with thick, colorful paint. Use this innovative practice pad for introducing letters, numerals, and geometric shapes. Concepts of over/under, right/left, top/bottom, and up/down are more readily understood through this visual and tactile experience.

Following Directions #1

After they have covered a sheet of paper with paint, have the children follow these verbal directions and answer the questions:

1. Draw a line across the middle of your paper. Draw a line down the middle of your paper. How many spaces do you have? Put an X in the right bottom space. Draw a heart shape in the top left space. Place four small circles in the top right space. Which space is empty?

2. Draw a line across the center of your paper. Make 2 triangles under the line. Make 4 thumb prints in the top space. Write your name on the line.

Following Directions #2

Older children can practice spelling words and multiplication tables. After they have covered a sheet of paper with paint, have them follow these verbal directions for math practice:

1. Write down the number of fingers on your right hand and subtract the number of thumbs you have.

2. Add the number of fingers on your right hand to the number of fingers on your friend's left hand.

3. Write 2 + 4 and then write the answer.

4. Write the answer to 4 × 5. Add 2 to that number.

Following Directions #3

Have children draw these surprise objects as you tell the following stories:

1. A large rectangle stopped to rest in the middle of your paper. One small circle rolled under the rectangle and stopped to rest at the left corner, touching the bottom of the rectangle. The circle's twin rolled under the other end of the rectangle and stopped to rest at the right corner, touching the bottom of the rectangle. A small square sat on the left top side of the rectangle. What did you make?

2. A big square sat at the bottom of your paper. A triangle sat on top of the big square. Along came a small rectangle. Where can you put it? What other shapes can you add?

Elaborate on each of these stories to meet the special needs of your own students. Practicing skills via finger painting provides students with the opportunity to create, alter, erase, and recreate. Finger painting is an old and fascinating art that can easily be integrated into all curriculum areas.

Chapter 2
Fundoughs for Pushing, Pounding, and Pinching

Creating with Fundoughs

Fundoughs are an excellent medium for stimulating creativity and imagination in young children. The experience of forming and manipulating objects of one's own creation is both soothing and satisfying. Working with dough mixtures also aids in developing fine motor skills and strengthens the muscles of the hands and fingers.

Fundoughs can be used to introduce and reinforce many concepts and basic skills. Children can use these creative doughs for forming letters, numerals, names, and shapes; for recognizing colors; for counting and grouping; and for discovering the concepts of large/small, more/less, up/down, and under/over.

Don't make models for the children. Let them discover on their own. Have the children practice rolling their palms back and forth on the table and rolling their palms together. Suggest that they move their palms forward, backward, and around. Have the children repeat the motions using the fundoughs. Children can create a wide variety of objects, starting with snakes and balls, by using these two motions.

While they are working with the doughs, have children sing this "Rolling Dough" song to the tune of "Row, Row, Row Your Boat."

Roll, roll, roll a snake.
Make it long and fat.
Roll it, roll it, roll it, roll it.
Roll it just like that.

Roll, roll, roll a ball.
Make it round and fat.
Roll it, roll it, roll it, roll it.
Roll it just like that.

To stimulate sensory awareness, have children add a pinch of powdered cloves or allspice, a few drops of lemon or almond extract, or a few drops of after-shave lotion to the dough mixture. A few drops of vinegar or oil of wintergreen or peppermint will retard spoilage and prevent unpleasant odors from developing.

Children will enjoy tinting dough by adding powdered tempera, squeeze-bottle liquid food coloring, or the paste colors used by cake decorators (these give a deeper color than tempera and food coloring). Powdered colors should be added to dry ingredients. Liquid colors should be added to water. If color is added after the dough is made, it is harder to work in and often leaves a marbled effect.

Colors will stain the hands; however, tinting the dough is a nice experience for the children to try.

Introduce tools only after children have had opportunities to roll, squeeze, pound, pinch, and create freely. Cookie cutters, a hand garlic press, plastic picnic knives and forks, and rolling pins or wooden dowels will provide another dimension for discovery.

Most homemade doughs keep well and can be stored in a container with a tight-fitting lid or in a plastic bag. If you want objects to harden, don't use recipes containing oil. Have children sun dry their finished products by placing the objects on a rack or on an inverted strawberry basket. This allows the air to circulate and to dry the undersides. For oven drying preheat to 350 degrees, set the figures on a rack, and turn off the oven.

Allow children to participate in making fundoughs by measuring, mixing, and kneading. Provide large spoons, plastic bowls, and measuring cups. Cooked fundoughs can be made in an electric frying pan. With supervision, a child can stir the mixture with a long-handled wooden spoon. Although the ingredients contained in these fundoughs are nontoxic, children should be discouraged from sampling the doughs. Recipes for edible doughs are included. Iodized salt can be used in these recipes, but do not use self-rising flour.

With extensive use, dough will become soiled and dry. Use old dough for forming sculptures. Plastic coffee can lids and foam meat trays make good bases. After dough hardens, it can be painted. Children will enjoy pressing shells, seeds, and other nature items into "mountains" or "pancakes" made from old dough. You can also recycle used dough by mixing it with water to form a special, one-time, squishy finger paint. Use a large tray or work outdoors.

Uncooked Fundoughs

Easy Fundough

1½ cups flour
¾ cup salt
¾ cup water

Supervise as you have children follow these steps:

1. Mix all ingredients together.
2. Slowly add more water if needed.
3. Knead until a workable dough is formed.

Easy Fundough (single portion)

4 tablespoons flour
2 tablespoons salt
3 tablespoons water

Supervise as you have children follow these steps:

1. Mix dry ingredients together.
2. Stir in the water.
3. Add more water or flour until dough forms a nonsticky ball.

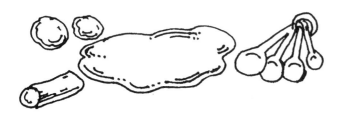

Salt, Flour, and Oil

3 cups flour
1 cup salt
3 tablespoons salad oil
1 cup water

Supervise as you have children follow these steps:

1. Mix dry ingredients together.
2. Stir in oil and water.
3. Add more water, as necessary, to form a soft, pliable dough.

This dough keeps well.

Salt, Flour, and Vinegar

3 cups flour
1 cup salt
1 cup water
¼ cup oil
2 tablespoons vinegar

Supervise as you have children follow these steps:

1. Mix all ingredients well. Add more water if necessary.
2. Knead.

This dough keeps indefinitely in a plastic bag. Dampen occasionally, working water into the dough as it dries out.

Salt, Flour, and Alum

1 cup salt

1 cup flour

1 teaspoon powdered alum
(available at drugstores,
nontoxic)

¾ cup water

Supervise as you have children
follow these steps:

1. Mix dry ingredients first.
2. Add half the water. If necessary,
   add more water to make the
   mixture stick together but not
   feel tacky.

This dough will harden to a good
permanent quality.

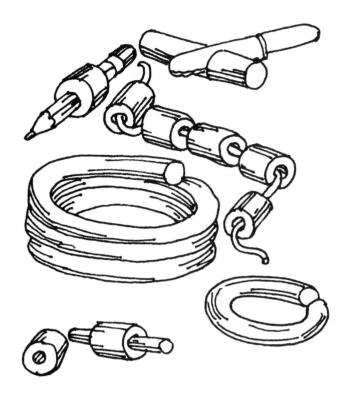

Cornmeal Dough

1½ cups flour

1½ cups cornmeal

1 cup salt

1 cup water

Supervise as you have children
follow these steps:

1. Mix all ingredients together.
2. Add more water to make the
   mixture cling.

This dough will keep up to six
weeks in an airtight container.

Coffee Grounds Dough

2 cups used, dry coffee grounds
½ cup salt
1½ cups cornmeal
warm water

Supervise as you have children follow these steps:

1. Mix dry ingredients together.
2. Add enough warm water to moisten.

This dough has a unique texture and is good to roll, pat, and pound.

Jewelry Clay

¾ cup flour
½ cup salt
½ cup cornstarch
warm water

Supervise as you have children follow these steps:

1. Mix dry ingredients together.
2. Gradually add warm water until the mixture can be kneaded into shapes.
3. Make beads by rolling the dough into little balls, piercing the balls with toothpicks, and allowing the balls to dry.
4. Paint and string the beads.

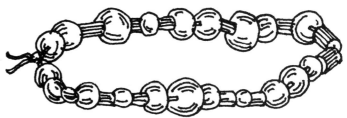

Soap Dough

    2 cups flour
    ½ cup salt
    2 tablespoons liquid paint
    1 tablespoon liquid soap
    water

Supervise as you have children follow these steps:

1. Mix all ingredients together.
2. Add water, as needed, to make a pliable dough.

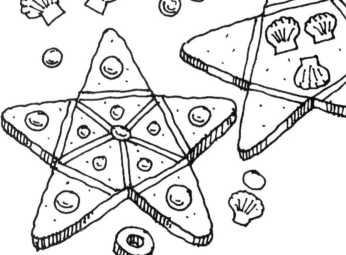

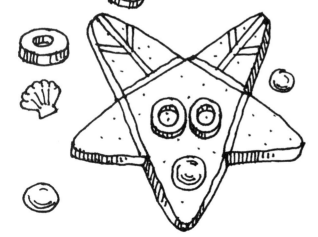

Cloud Dough

    3 cups flour
    2 tablespoons powdered tempera
    ½ cup salad oil
    water

Supervise as you have children follow these steps:

1. Mix together the flour, tempera, and oil.
2. Add enough water to make a soft, pliable, elastic-like dough.

This dough does not keep well.

Glue Dough

1 cup flour
1 cup cornstarch
½ cup white liquid glue
water

Supervise as you have children follow these steps:

1. Mix all ingredients together.
2. Add water as needed.
3. Knead until workable.

Cooked Fundoughs

Make cooked fundoughs in the classroom. Use an electric skillet and a long-handled spoon. For recipes that require boiling water, an electric teapot and a mixing bowl would be useful. Cooking activities should be supervised by an adult. Allow fundoughs to cool before the children use them.

Flour and Salt

1 cup flour
1 cup salt
1 cup water

Supervise as you have children follow these steps:

1. Mix ingredients in an electric skillet.
2. Stir on a low heat setting until the mixture is thick.
3. Let cool.

Flour, Salt, and Cream of Tartar

1 cup flour
½ cup salt
2 teaspoons cream of tartar
1 cup water
1 tablespoon salad oil

Supervise as you have children follow these steps:

1. Mix all ingredients together in an electric skillet.
2. Cook on a low heat setting until the mixture is lumpy.
3. Turn the dough out on wax paper.
4. Knead when cool.

This dough has an excellent quality, keeps well, and does not crumble.

Sugar and Flour

1 cup sugar
1 cup flour
1 cup cold water
5 cups boiling water

Supervise as you have children follow these steps:

1. Mix the first 3 ingredients in an electric skillet.
2. Add boiling water and cook for 5 minutes, stirring constantly.
3. Cool.

This dough does not keep very well.

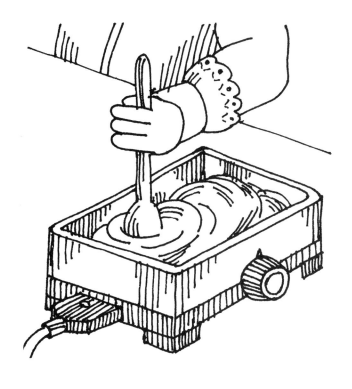

Cornstarch and Salt #1

4 cups salt
1 cup cornstarch
water

Supervise as you have children follow these steps:

1. Combine salt and cornstarch in an electric skillet.
2. Add enough water to form a paste.
3. Cook on a medium heat setting, stirring constantly.

This dough will not be sticky like flour dough and will not mold because of the high salt content.

Cornstarch and Salt #2

2 cups salt

⅔ cup water

1 cup cornstarch

½ cup additional water

Supervise as you have children follow these steps:

1. In an electric skillet, mix the salt with ⅔ cup water.
2. Cook on a medium setting for 4 to 5 minutes. Turn heat off.
3. In a bowl, mix together the cornstarch and ½ cup cold water. Stir this into the cooked mixture until smooth.
4. Cook on a medium heat setting until the mixture is thick.
5. Cool.

This dough can be dried and painted. It will not crumble.

Flour and Cornstarch

½ cup flour

1 cup cornstarch

2½ cups water

¼ teaspoon baking soda

Supervise as you have children follow these steps:

1. In an electric skillet, mix all ingredients together.
2. Cook on a low heat setting until the mixture forms a workable dough.
3. Cool and knead.

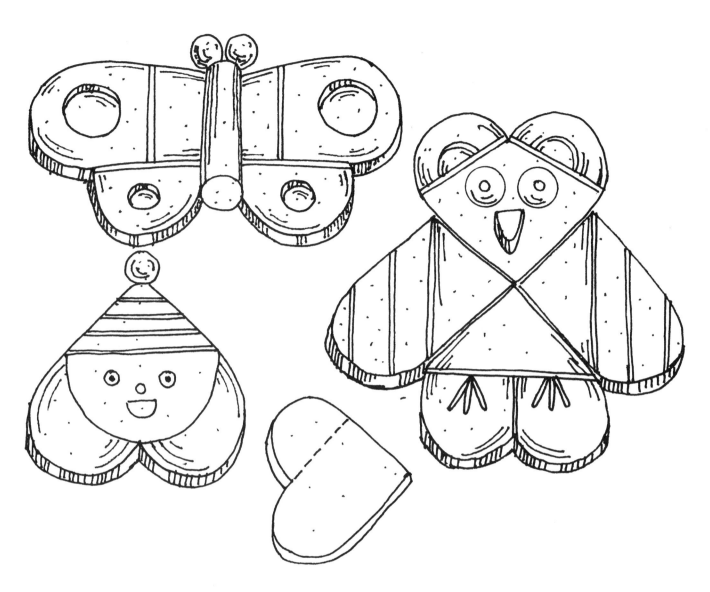

Cornstarch and Soda

½ cup cornstarch
½ cup plus 2 tablespoons water
1 cup baking soda

Supervise as you have children follow these steps:

1. Combine ingredients in an electric skillet.
2. Stir while cooking until the mixture is thick and doughlike.
3. When cool, knead.

Edible Fundoughs

All edible fundoughs should be made, used, and eaten the same day.

Peanut Butter and Syrup

1 cup peanut butter
1 cup corn syrup
1½ cups powdered sugar
1½ cups powdered milk

Supervise as you have children follow these steps:

1. Mix all ingredients together with a spoon.
2. Add more powdered milk if necessary to make a workable dough.
3. Knead, shape, and eat.

Peanut Butter and Honey

1 cup peanut butter
1 cup honey
2 cups powdered milk

Supervise as you have children follow these steps:

1. Mix all ingredients together in a bowl.
2. Add more powdered milk if necessary to make a workable dough.
3. Form the dough into balls and other shapes.

Frosting Fundough	Oatmeal Fundough
1 can frosting mix 1½ cups powdered sugar 1 cup peanut butter Have children mix all ingredients together until they form a workable dough.	2 cups uncooked oatmeal 1 cup flour ¼ cup water Have children mix all ingredients together and knead the dough. This dough is not very tasty.

Fundough Treat

¼ cup brown sugar

¼ cup peanut butter

1 tablespoon granola (optional)

Supervise as you have children follow these steps:

1. Measure the brown sugar and the peanut butter into a plastic bowl.
2. Squeeze mixture with both hands. (This is a special tactile experience that children love!)
3. If the mixture is too sticky, add a little more brown sugar. If it is too dry, add more peanut butter.
4. Add granola, if desired, for extra interest and nutrition.

Allow children time to enjoy the mixing process before they shape this treat into balls and other forms.

Spice Fundough

2 cups flour

2 teaspoons baking powder

⅓ cup sugar

½ teaspoon salt

½ teaspoon cinnamon

¼ teaspoon nutmeg

⅓ cup milk

4 tablespoons salad oil

Supervise as you have children follow these steps:

1. Mix the dry ingredients together.
2. Add milk and oil.
3. Knead until dough sticks together and forms a ball.
4. Divide dough into portions on wax paper sheets.
5. Roll and shape the mixture into doughnut shapes or other forms.

This dough can be fried in oil at 375 degrees. If dough is to be used for play, substitute water for the milk. This dough has a nice texture, an unusual appearance, and a spicy aroma.

Bread Fundough

½ cup hot water

½ cup canned evaporated milk

1 teaspoon salt

2 tablespoons sugar

2 tablespoons oil

½ package dry yeast dissolved in 2 additional tablespoons warm water

3 cups flour

raisins (optional)

Supervise as you have children follow these steps:

1. Mix together all ingredients except the flour and raisins.

2. Stir in 2 cups flour.

3. Add more flour until dough leaves the sides of the bowl and can be kneaded.

4. Divide into portions. (Each child should receive a portion on a sheet of wax paper dusted with flour.)

5. Continue kneading single portions until dough becomes springy. Add raisins if desired, and knead them in.

6. Let the dough rise until double in size. Knead it down again.

7. Let it rise for a second time. Knead it down again.

8. Shape dough into balls or other forms.

9. Place shapes onto an oiled pan and let them rise again until double in size.

10. Bake at 375 degrees until lightly brown.

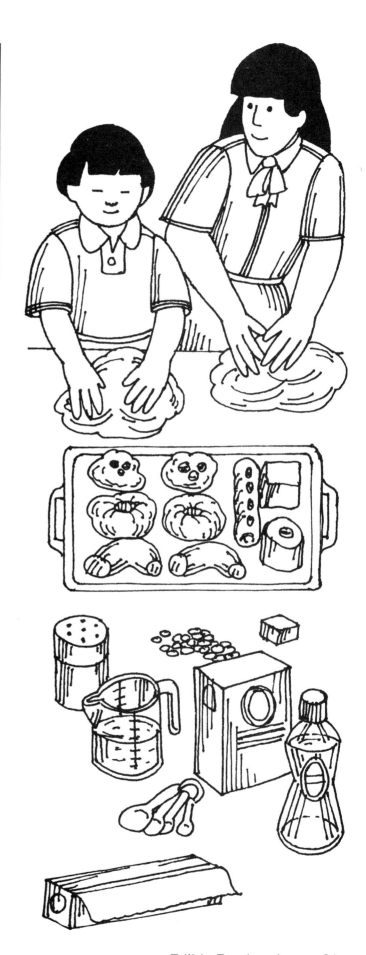

Extended Uses for Fundoughs

Use fundoughs for introducing and reinforcing concepts. Make a workboard for each child using a 9″ × 12″ piece of cardboard. Cover with plastic wrap or adhesive-backed paper.

Provide a board and a portion of fundough for each child. Have younger children form the dough into letters, numerals, geometric shapes, or holiday symbols. Have them make 3 or 4 balls, each a different shape. Next, have them place the balls in order from largest to smallest and from smallest to largest.

Instruct children to roll out a long rope of fundough and place it across the center of the board. Have them make the remaining dough into small balls. Give the following instructions for placement of the balls: "Place 2 balls over the rope; place 3 balls under the rope; set 1 ball on the rope." Have the children make another rope and place it vertically. Give directions for placing balls in upper right, upper left, bottom right, and bottom left spaces.

Provide children with several different colors of dough. Make matching tagboard squares. Hold up a color and ask children to find the matching dough color. Add outline shapes, letters, or other simple objects on the cards. Hold up a card and ask the children to duplicate the form with dough. If children are unable to form the shapes, draw the shapes on the workboards before covering them with plastic wrap.

Using scissors is a good activity for developing fine motor control. Have children practice using scissors by cutting pieces from a long, thin rope of fundough. When they are successful, ask them to cut 2 small pieces and 2 large pieces.

Make pattern cards showing colored balls for the children to duplicate with dough. You might show 3 red balls, 1 yellow ball, and 2 blue balls. Have children make dough balls in a variety of colors, push holes through the centers with toothpicks, and then set them out to dry. Then have the children string the balls on yarn in the same pattern as you have on the pattern cards.

Give older children practice in measuring and understanding fractions by providing them with a large piece of dough, a ruler, a workboard, paper, and a pencil. Have them roll out a snake 12 inches long. Have them measure and cut the snake into 2 equal pieces. Have the children record the length of each piece. Then have them cut each of the 2 pieces into 3 pieces. Ask, "How long is each piece?" Have children total the length of all pieces. Ask, "Does the total equal the length of the original piece?" Have children put the original 12-inch snake back together. Then have them cut it into quarters or thirds.

For grouping and simple math practice, fundough can provide a tangible tool. Have children make some small dough balls. Then have them each take 2 balls and set them aside. Have each child add 4 more balls to the original 2. Ask, "How many do you have now?" Help children relate this to the equation 2 + 4 = 6. Subtraction and multiplication examples can be practiced in the same way.

Use a felt pen to divide a piece of cardboard into 6 equal pieces. Number the spaces 1 through 6. Cover the board with clear plastic wrap. Have children make the designated number of balls and place them in the correct spaces.

Try this math activity. Give each child a portion of edible dough. Have each child make 8 tiny balls. Then have each child write the numbers 1 through 8 across a sheet of clean paper. Then say, "Place one ball below each number." Give the following directions or create your own: "Eat number 3 and number 7. Eat number 1. How many did you eat? How many are left? How many more must you eat in order to have 3 remaining? Eat the first and last remaining balls. Which balls are left? Eat the center ball. Eat the ball on the left. How many balls have you eaten? How many balls are left? What should you do with it?" This activity also works well on a one-to-one basis with a child who needs extra help.

Chapter 3
Molding Mixtures

What Are Molding Mixtures?

This chapter provides a variety of unusual materials that can be molded into objects, puppets, ornaments, and decorations. These activities will present interesting challenges to young artists as they experience the magic of creating from raw materials.

Sawdust should be strained so it is free of splinters. Ask a cabinetmaker or a lumberyard worker to save sawdust for you.

You can make puppet heads from sawdust dough or from papier-mâché by molding the material around your index finger. Mold and shape a form as desired, remove it from your finger, and let it dry. Then, roll a piece of paper around your finger and glue it to the inside of the puppet head, letting the paper extend about an inch below the neck. Glue the puppet costume to the paper.

Mixtures to Mold

Molding Flakes

1 cup soap flakes*
¼ cup water
* If you are unable to find soap flakes, make your own with a kitchen vegetable grater and a bar of Ivory soap.

Supervise as you have children follow these steps:

1. Add half the water to the soap flakes.
2. Beat with a rotary eggbeater until the mixture has a flaky appearance. Add more water if necessary.
3. Mold as desired.

This dough has a nice texture, but it takes a long time to dry.

Molding Dough (cooked)

1 cup salt
⅓ cup water
½ cup cornstarch
¼ cup cold water

Supervise as you have children follow these steps:

1. Mix salt and ⅓ cup water in an electric skillet.
2. Cook on a medium heat setting, stirring constantly until the mixture comes to a boil. Turn the heat off.
3. In a bowl, mix cornstarch and ¼ cup cold water together until smooth.
4. Add cornstarch mixture to the cooked mixture, and turn the heat back on.
5. Cook the mixture until it is thick. Cool before molding.

Sawdust and Flour

4 cups sawdust (strained)
2 cups flour
1 cup water
2 tablespoons white liquid glue

Supervise as you have children follow these steps:

1. Mix sawdust and flour.
2. Gradually add water until the dough holds together.
3. Before forming objects for drying and painting, add 2 tablespoons of white liquid glue.

Sawdust and Wheat Paste

2 cups sawdust (strained)
1 cup wheat paste or wallpaper paste
½ cup water

Supervise as you have children follow these steps:

1. Mix sawdust and paste.
2. Add only enough water to make the mixture pliable.

This dough responds better to squeezing and shaping than to rolling and patting.

Sawdust and Plaster of Paris

2 cups sawdust (strained)
1 cup plaster of paris
½ cup wallpaper paste
2 cups water

Supervise as you have children follow these steps:

1. Mix the first three ingredients together.
2. Slowly add water until you have a workable dough.

Papier-Mâché

newspapers
water
liquid laundry starch, thick water and flour paste, wheat paste, liquid glue, or old library paste diluted with water

Supervise as you have children follow these steps:

1. Tear newspapers into very small pieces.
2. Soak the pieces in a pan of hot water.
3. Squeeze out the excess water until the newspaper becomes pulpy.
4. Add a small amount of one of the following: liquid laundry starch, thick water and flour paste, wheat paste, liquid glue, or old library paste diluted with water.

Use papier-mâché for free molding or mold it around an existing shape such as a jar, a can, a box, or a crumpled wad of newspaper.

Tissue Pulp

tissues (white or colored)
liquid starch
liquid glue

Supervise as you have children follow these steps:

1. Tear tissues into strips.
2. Soak the strips in liquid starch until they are mushy.
3. Add a little liquid glue so the pulp will hold its form when it is dry.
4. Form the mixture into a ball and squeeze out excess starch.
5. Shape as desired.

If you use white tissues, you may wish to paint the finished form when it is thoroughly dry.

Crepe Paper Clay

3½ cups crepe paper (white or colored)
water
1 cup flour
½ cup salt
3 drops vanilla extract (to counteract the unpleasant odor)

Supervise as you have children follow these steps:

1. Cut crepe paper into small strips.
2. Soak strips in water.
3. Squeeze out most of the water.
4. Add flour, salt, and vanilla.
5. Knead and mold.

Colored crepe paper will stain the hands. White crepe paper can be painted when it is dry.

Glue Dough

¾ cup flour

¼ cup white liquid glue

¼ cup thick liquid shampoo

Supervise as you have children follow these steps:

1. Combine all ingredients in a bowl.
2. Knead. Add more flour if needed.
3. Roll out, shape, or cut into designs.

This dough can be painted when dry.

Puff Dough

1 cup flour

¾ to 1 cup water

1 bag small cotton balls

Supervise as you have children follow these steps:

1. Mix flour and water together until you have a smooth, thick paste.
2. Coat the cotton balls with the paste. They tend to puff up and will remain puffed up if you handle them gently.
3. Carefully lift each cotton ball from the mixture, allowing excess to drop off.
4. Form the cotton balls into desired shapes on a nonstick cookie sheet.
5. Bake in an oven at 325 degrees for about an hour or until the shapes are lightly browned and hard to the touch.

When the shapes are cool, they can be painted.

Clothespin Character

4 tablespoons flour
2 tablespoons salt
water
1 all-wood clothespin

Supervise as you have children follow these steps:

1. Mix flour and water together.
2. Slowly add enough water to form a moldable dough.
3. Cover the top of the clothespin with the dough. Shape or mold as desired. Make indentations for eyes and pull out dough for ears and nose.
4. Slip the clothespin over the rim of a deep baking pan.
5. Bake the figure for about an hour in an oven at 325 degrees.

This clothespin character can be painted when cool.

Bread Molding Dough

8 slices stale white bread
8 tablespoons white liquid glue
2 teaspoons glycerine

Supervise as you have children follow these steps:

1. Remove crusts from bread and discard them.
2. Crumble the bread into a bowl.
3. Add glue and 1 teaspoon glycerine. Mix well.
4. Pour the remaining glycerine into your hands and knead the dough well.
5. Place the dough into a plastic bag and allow it to set overnight.

This dough can be molded or cut into designs.

Chapter 4
Special Mixtures

What Makes Cornstarch So Special?

Cornstarch and water is an easy-to-prepare mixture that children will find intriguing and fun to play with. Have them scoop it up with their hands and allow it to run back into the bowl. They will see that it flows fairly easily. Then have them push their fists into it. They will see that it doesn't splash like other fluids. Since the mixture behaves like both a solid and a liquid, it provides a sensory-tactile experience that is unequaled.

Fun with Cornstarch

Cornstarch Magic

½ cup cornstarch
¼ cup water
food coloring
teaspoon
margarine tub

Supervise as you have children follow these steps:

1. Place cornstarch into margarine tub.
2. Slowly add water, 1 teaspoon at a time, and stir. Feel the mixture with your hands.
3. Continue adding water, 1 teaspoon at a time, until the mixture is a thick paste. Observe the changes in the mixture as you add water.
4. Pick up the mixture. Squeeze it. Open your hand and let it ooze through your fingers.
5. Without mixing them in, add 3 drops of food coloring. Observe as the food coloring disperses through the mixture.

Overnight Changes

1 box cornstarch
1 cup water
extra cornstarch

Supervise as you have children follow these steps:

1. Empty box of cornstarch into a plastic bowl.

2. Add ¼ cup water. Stir carefully with a long-handled wooden spoon.

3. Slowly add more water and observe the changes in the mixture.

4. When you have finished experimenting, set the mixture aside and leave it overnight.

5. The next day, observe the mixture. (It will appear to be dry and caked.) Stir it well. Slowly add more water. Then add more cornstarch. Observe what happens as you alternately add cornstarch and water.

Pedi-Squish

2 parts cornstarch
1 part water

Supervise as you have children follow these steps:

1. Mix cornstarch and water in a flat pan. (Size of pan will determine amount of cornstarch and water required. The ratio of the ingredients should always be 2 parts cornstarch to 1 part water.)

2. Sit in chairs and place your bare feet into the mixture.

3. Wiggle your toes, press your feet down hard, and raise one foot.

4. Stand up, and walk in place.

This is a valuable sensory experience for all children, but especially young children and those with handicaps.

Mud Pies and More

What ever happened to mud pies? Few of today's children have had the joy of experimenting with plain mud. Yet this is probably the oldest form of sculpturing and the first of all creative art mixtures. Don't let your students miss out on marvelous mud molding experiences.

If possible, work outside with mud mixtures. Mud mixtures also work well indoors at a water table, in a heavy plastic wading pool, or in a large dishpan.

Magic with Mud

Mud Dough

2 cups dirt (free of pebbles)
water

Supervise as you have children follow these steps:

1. Mix the dirt with enough water to form mud that will hold together. If possible, mix the mud in a hole in the yard.
2. Pat the mud dough out to a thickness of about ¼ inch.
3. Use plastic knives to cut the mud dough into various shapes. Make farm animals, people, vehicles, or simple geometric shapes.
4. Dry the figures in the sun on a rack, and use them for outdoor play.

Mud Dough Variations

For added interest, have children try the following:

1. Add either ½ cup of sand or ½ cup of salt to 2 cups of mud. This mixture will not hold its form as well as the basic mud dough recipe. When this is dry, notice the difference in textures.
2. Use clay soil instead of plain dirt for the basic mud dough recipe. This mixture works well for sculpturing. Have a bowl of water nearby so you can keep your hands wet as you sculpt.

Starting with Sand

Sand Dough (cooked)

1 cup sand (strained)
½ cup cornstarch
¾ cup hot water
wax paper

Supervise as you have children follow these steps:

1. Mix ingredients in an electric skillet.
2. Cook mixture on a low heat setting, stirring with a long-handled wooden spoon until it has a doughlike consistency.
3. Spoon out onto wax paper.
4. When it is cool, knead and mold the dough as desired.
5. Set the finished figures out in the sun to dry.

Castles can be made directly on the ground or formed on a large piece of corrugated cardboard.

To stimulate the imagination of young castle builders, provide a box of assorted items such as ice-cream sticks, pieces of fabric, Styrofoam pieces, shells, and other decorations. Children can make individual castles and plan and hold an art show. Extend the activity by having them research castles of the Middle Ages. You may want to involve the entire school by having each class construct a replica of a different castle. Invite parents to view the finished products.

Sand Castles to Keep

6 cups sand
1 cup wheat paste
water
paper cups, tin cans, plastic food containers, clay flower pots, drinking straws, flags, and other decorations

Supervise as you have children follow these steps:

1. Mix wheat paste and sand.
2. Add water until the sand has a claylike consistency. It should be sticky, and it should pack firmly into shapes. More sand and water may be added as needed. The wetter the sand, the longer it will take to dry.
3. Use any large container as a base for your castle. Pack the sand firmly around the base and add turrets shaped from paper cups or other small containers. Use sticks or plastic utensils to form windows, steps, and other designs.

Plaster, Mortar, Molds, and Plaques

Plaster of Paris Projects

Plaster of Paris Molds
plaster of paris water food coloring (optional) plastic coffee can lids shells, rocks, leaves, and other decorations Supervise as you have children follow these steps: 1. Mix plaster of paris according to the directions on the package. Tint with food coloring if desired. 2. Pour the mixture into plastic coffee can lids. 3. Add shells, rocks, leaves, and other decorations. 4. Let dry.

Painting Board
plaster of paris water wood or heavy cardboard paint Supervise as you have children follow these steps: 1. Mix plaster of paris according to the directions on the package. 2. Use a tongue depressor to spread the mixture onto a thin piece of wood or a piece of heavy cardboard. Cover completely with a thin layer. 3. When the plaster of paris is dry, paint a scene or design on it.

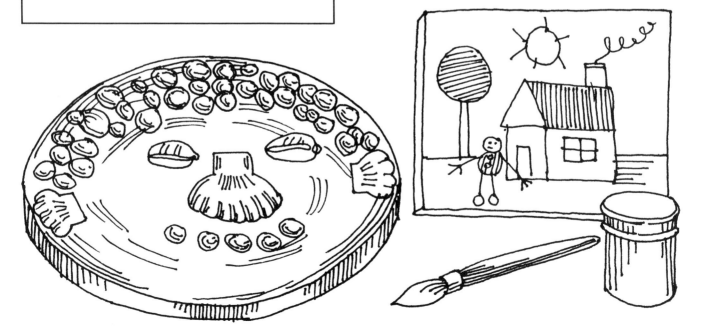

Creating with Cement

Mortar

1 part cement

1 part builder's sand

water

paper plate, plastic lid, or small foil pan

rocks, shells, or other decorations

Supervise as you have children follow these steps:

1. Mix together equal amounts of sand and cement, using a small garden shovel or a metal spoon (don't use your hands).

2. Add enough water to form a nice workable mixture.

3. Pour into a paper plate, plastic lid, or small foil pan.

4. Drop in rocks, shells, or other decorations.

5. Smooth with a tongue depressor.

6. **Wash all utensils immediately with cold water. Mortar and concrete can be washed off your hands by using full-strength vinegar.**

This is a fascinating experience for the children.

Footprint Stepping-Stone (Concrete)

1 part cement*
2 parts builder's sand*
3 parts small pebbles*
water
cooking oil
* Check with a local building supply store to see if they are willing to donate concrete materials.

Make a reusable frame by nailing 4 pieces of 12″ × 2″ board together to form a 12″ square. Set the frame on a dirt surface or on a piece of heavy foil. If you don't wish to make a frame, you can use a shoe box for each child.

Supervise as you have children follow these steps:

1. Use a small garden shovel or metal spoon to mix together the first 3 ingredients.

2. Add enough water to make a very wet mixture.

3. Pour the concrete into the mold.

4. Use a tongue depressor to smooth the surface.

5. Rub oil on the bottom and sides of your foot.

6. Press foot into the concrete to make a good print.

7. Take foot out of the concrete, wash it immediately in cold water, and then wash it in vinegar.

8. Use a nail to sign and date the footprint.

9. Let concrete set until firm.

10. Remove frame for reuse. Let footprint dry completely.

You may want to undertake a larger project by making a giant stepping-stone somewhere in the school yard. You will need the cooperation of the school principal, a custodian, and a volunteer parent or two. Let the children help you plan, estimate, and purchase needed materials. Ready-mix concrete can be purchased at any building supply store. Coloring is also available for tinting the mixture. Construct the frame, prepare the ground, and mix and pour the concrete. You may wish to have children put signed and dated handprints around the edges of the slab. Check with a local building supply store about borrowing tools to "finish" the concrete.

Hand Plaques

Plaster of Paris Hand Plaque

plaster of paris
water
foil pan
cooking oil

Supervise as you have children follow these steps:

1. Mix plaster of paris according to the directions on the package.

2. Pour the mixture into a foil pan.

3. Rub one hand with cooking oil and press it firmly into the center of the pan.

4. Remove hand from plaster of paris and wash it immediately.

5. When the plaster of paris is partly set, use a pencil to make a small hole near the top of the plaque for hanging.

Clay Mold

clay

plaster of paris

water

paint

Supervise as you have children follow these steps:

1. Pound out a piece of clay, about an inch thick, into a shape larger than your hand.

2. Press hand into clay very firmly. Press hard on that hand with your other hand to make a good print.

3. Remove hand from clay and wash it.

4. Mix plaster of paris according to the directions on the package.

5. Fill clay handprint with plaster of paris mixture.

6. When the plaster of paris is dry, peel off the clay and brush off the handprint to remove any remaining traces of clay.

7. Paint the handprint as desired.

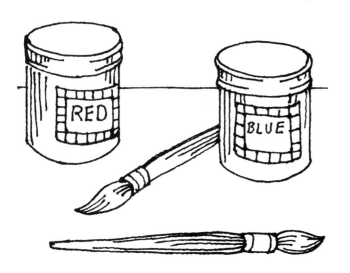

Sand Mold

sand

water

plaster of paris

paint

Supervise as you have children follow these steps:

1. Pour sand into a box or pan.

2. Add water and mix until all the sand is wet.

3. Press your hand into the sand until you have a good print.

4. Remove your hand from the sand and wash it.

5. Mix plaster of paris according to the directions on the package.

6. Fill the print in the sand with the plaster of paris mixture.

7. When the plaster of paris is dry, lift the handprint out and brush off the sand.

8. Paint as desired.

Salt and Flour Print (cooked)

½ cup flour

¼ cup salt

¼ cup water

paint

yarn or ribbon

Supervise as you have children follow these steps:

1. Mix salt and flour.
2. Slowly add water.
3. Knead dough for a few minutes.
4. Using a rolling pin, roll out to about ¼″ thick and into a circle or an oval.
5. Press hand into dough to make a deep print. If you like, you may cut around the hand outline with a plastic knife.
6. Use a pencil to make a small hole in the top.
7. Place the handprint on a piece of aluminum foil and bake it in an oven at 325 degrees until it is light brown. The handprint can also be air dried overnight or sun dried.
8. When the handprint is cool, paint as desired.
9. String a piece of yarn or ribbon through the hole for hanging.

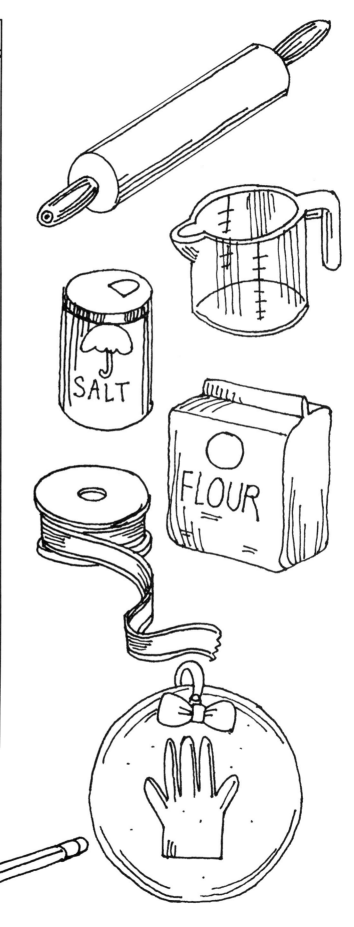

Mud Print

dirt (Clay earth is best.)

water

Supervise as you have children follow these steps:

1. Add water to dirt to make a thick mud.
2. Flatten the mud out to about ¼" thick.
3. Press hand into the mud to make a print.
4. Remove hand from the mud and wash it.
5. Use a plastic knife to cut around the outline of the print, if desired.
6. Allow print to dry in the sun.

Chapter 5

Miscellaneous Mixture Ideas

Flour + Water = ?

Flour plus water is an interesting combination for making both paste and paint mixtures.

Make your own paste by mixing a little flour and a little water until the mixture is sticky and pastelike.

Make your own finger paint by mixing a little flour and a little water together. Beat with a spoon until the mixture is thick and creamy.

Make your own paint by mixing a little flour and a little water. Make a thin mixture and stir until all the lumps disappear. Use for brush painting.

Add red food coloring to any of these mixtures for Valentine's Day, green food coloring for St. Patrick's Day, and red and green food coloring for Christmas. At Easter, let the children experiment with the three basic colors to tint their own paint and paste mixtures.

Liquid Starch Art

Rolled Beads

12 long triangles cut from
newsprint (see pattern)
bowl of liquid starch
12″ square of wax paper
paint
yarn

Supervise as you have children
follow these steps:

1. Dip a newsprint triangle into
the starch.
2. Remove it, and let the excess
starch drip off.
3. Starting at the pointed end, roll
the triangle around the pencil.
4. Slip the rolled bead off onto the
wax paper.
5. Repeat steps 1–4 until all the
beads are made.
6. When the beads are dry, paint
them.
7. String the beads onto a piece of
yarn.

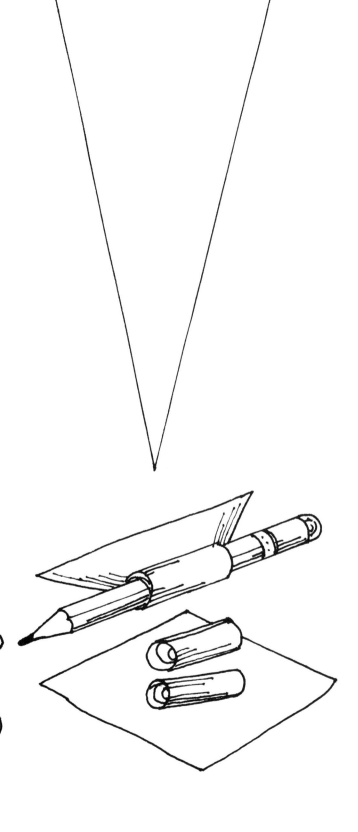

Starch Hangings

liquid starch
2 12″ squares of wax paper
white liquid glue (optional)
miscellaneous flat items (leaves,
   petals, decorative paper, fabric)
string

Supervise as you have children follow these steps:

1. Use either your hand or a paint brush to cover a sheet of wax paper with liquid starch.

2. Arrange flat items on the starch.

3. Top with a second sheet of wax paper, press lightly, and let dry overnight. If you add a little bit of white liquid glue to the starch, it will hasten drying.

4. When the starch is completely dry, use a hole punch to make a hole at the top through both layers of wax paper. Add a string, and hang it in a window.

5. If you would like to trim the paper or cut it into a geometric shape, use pinking shears.

Net Molds

small balloons
petroleum jelly
yarn in assorted colors
liquid starch

Inflate the balloons to the desired size and knot the ends. Have children work in pairs. One child can hold the balloon while the other child completes the following steps:

1. Completely cover the balloon with a thin coat of petroleum jelly.
2. Dip lengths of yarn into the liquid starch.
3. Wrap the starch-soaked yarn around the balloon at various angles to create a net effect.
4. Set the balloon on wax paper.
5. When the starch is completely dry, carefully puncture the balloon and remove it.

Use these net molds for Christmas decorations, or hang them in a sunny window. To make Easter eggs, use oval-shaped balloons.

Magic Mixtures

Creative Fun for Little Ones

Is there a child in the world who doesn't love to play with dough? Finger paints? Mud and other wonderfully plastic things? *Magic Mixtures: Creative Fun for Little Ones* is full of recipes for all kinds of marvelous mixtures your children will love to jump right into.

There are also super suggestions for teaching many valuable skills through manipulation of the mixtures. Your children will enjoy creating shapes and pictures and they will gain essential experiences with measuring ingredients, mixing, kneading, molding, and cleaning up. Children will work with textures and they will learn what happens when substances are combined. They can experiment with such delightful materials as flour, starch, salt, gelatin, frosting, tempera, food coloring, peanut butter, corn syrup, sand, plaster of paris, and even cement.

All recipes use simple, easy-to-find ingredients, and contain detailed directions for preparation along with solid teaching suggestions. Help your youngsters develop important coordination skills and basic concepts (great works of art, too!) with lessons that make use of the magic of mixtures.

Preschool–Grade 3

Other books by Jean Stangl

Paper Stories, #5402

Fingerlings: Finger Puppet Fun for Little Ones, #3061

FlannelGraphs: Flannel Board Fun for Little Ones, #3060

For a complete catalog, write:
Fearon Teacher Aids
P.O. Box 280
Carthage, Illinois 62321

ISBN 0-8224-4377-5